Bipolar Disorder

A Guide to Understanding, Managing, and Treating Bipolar Disorder

Jessica Rose

Table of Contents

Introduction 1

Chapter 1: What Is Bipolar Disorder? 3

Chapter 2: Treatment and Assistance 20

Chapter 3: Alternative Treatments 35

Chapter 4: Brave New World 46

Chapter 5: Age and Gender 60

Conclusion 77

Introduction

Congratulations, and thank you so much for choosing this book as a method to learn about one of the most widespread and misunderstood mental illnesses that exists. Throughout the following chapters, we will take a closer look at Bipolar Disorder and the way it changes the lives of both the sufferer and their loved ones.

The history of treatment for mental illnesses is a dark record of ignorance and misunderstanding. There is so much left to learn, even in the modern era. As our knowledge of the subject expands, so does the way we care for those that have been diagnosed. Bipolar Disorder carries one of the highest risks of mortality, which necessitates drastic action to aid those who have been affected by it.

We will soon discuss all the available treatment options for Bipolar Disorder. As you will learn, medication and Therapy are an excellent foundation from which to build. Innovative alternatives are also beginning to make their way into the public consciousness.

Did you know that most people who suffer from Bipolar Disorder will never receive the correct diagnosis? Of those who are correctly identified, many will never receive the appropriate care.

I hope that this book will open your eyes to the realities of Bipolar Disorder, and how it can be managed and controlled. Finally, I urge you to never self-diagnose, or to diagnose a loved one. If after reading this book you feel that you may be suffering from Bipolar Disorder, I encourage you to seek the services of a mental health professional to make an accurate diagnosis.

Once again, thank you for taking the time to read this book. I hope you find it to be both informative, and helpful.

Chapter 1: What Is Bipolar Disorder?

Mental health has not always been a topic that society freely discussed. Illnesses and disorders of the mind have been covered in a thick shroud of stigma and ambiguity. Fortunately, advancements in our understanding of psychology have drastically changed the way we view and treat neurodiversity.

Bipolar Disorder (or BP) has made an imprint on human history, and one must imagine the tribulation endured by early sufferers. The first known observation associated with the condition occurred during the first century of our current record. Aretaeus of Cappadocia discovered that depressive episodes and mania were just two sides of the same illness.

If we were to follow the timeline even further back, Hippocrates, the father of medicine and the reason for the Hippocratic oath, characterized symptoms of mania and depression. During his lifetime (460-337 BCE), Hippocrates studied mood and personality, attempting to relate it back to the humors of the body. The word melancholia was a meshing of the two words "black" and "bile" in the Ancient Greek language. What is believed to have been Bipolar Disorder was treated with water that doctors believed to have healing properties.

Ancient Greece laid the blueprint for societal advancement during their time, inspiring nations all throughout the human timeline and across the globe. History was not always so progressive when it came to interpreting scientific and medical data. In fact, following the enlightenment of Hippocrates and Aretaeus, psychology took a nosedive.

For centuries, the response to mania was less "treat the patient" and more "burn the witch." Those with mental illnesses, disorders, or anomalies were regarded as being possessed by demons in the not-so-distant past. The shameful treatment of neurodiversity did not end there.

Human history slowly inched past the need to describe every illness as demonic possession. The eighteenth and early nineteenth century found an equally harmful way to deal with society's vulnerable populations. Asylums became commonplace as patients were subjected to brutal "treatments" in unsupervised facilities that existed more for-profit than to serve a general good.

In the middle of the nineteenth century, a man named Jean-Pierre Falret gave form to the illness. In 1850, Falret wrote an article relating mania to depression, also observing that the condition seemed to run in families. Early Bipolar Disorder was known as circular insanity. Twenty-five years later, the Disorder was updated to be called Manic Depressive Psychosis.

One may have believed that with these advancements being made, the story of Bipolar Disorder was finally on track to become a bit less dark. Sadly, during the 1900's electroshock therapy and lobotomies still cast a bleak light over the field of psychology; the latter was popular until the 1960s. Later within that same decade, the narrative finally changed.

In 1968 Bipolar Disorder was reclassified as Manic-Depressive Illness. Leaps and bounds were being made in the fields of psychology and pharmacology; heinous treatments resembling torture methods from the dark ages were on their way out. The seventies saw several legislative protections implemented for patients with mental illnesses.

The Americans with Disabilities Act was authored in the 1990s, a harbinger for shifting attitudes toward mental illness and neurodiversity. The landscape was finally changing in a meaningful way. Individuals with treatable disorders were no longer going to be incapacitated before their lives even began. The horrors of the previous decades now stand behind us, like a monolith, a reminder of the price of ignorance.

What Is Bipolar Disorder

Emotions and moods are variations of the same idea. Emotions are more fluid feelings that pass from one moment to the next. You might be sad for a day, only to bounce back when you awaken on the following sunny morning. Our minds react to changing stimuli with similarly evolving responses.

The mood is a more long-term state of feeling, and it is also much less intense than an emotion. Think back to the last time you were in a bad mood. Were you immediately aware that you were not pleased? Did it take a little while to notice the tension or nagging sadness?

Moods also tend to inform our emotions. Think back again to your last lousy mood. Did your general unease cause you anger, frustration, or sadness? Fleeting feelings heavily depend upon our predispositions.

BP is a mental illness that drastically changes the life and emotional state of the sufferer. The condition is characterized by severe and sudden changes in mood, from euphoric highs (mania) to depressive lows (depression). Extremes may occur one after the other, or both at the same time. Mania is an elevated and excitable mood that might produce a euphoric high but could also be deeply unpleasant. The individual might act entirely outside of their usual character because they are compelled by impulses that they cannot control.

We will dive deeper into mania shortly, but, for now, imagine an individual who has an unending amount of energy coursing through their veins; they don't need sleep or food as they might during a more stable mood. Manic people speak fast and move with haste from one project to the next. This high could last anywhere from a few days to whole years. There are plenty of negative aspects to having an uncontrollably energetic mood.

Depressive episodes are characterized by a low-energy mood. The suffering individual needs to always sleep and may stay in bed for days. Productivity falls to almost nothing as completing assignments can feel like hellish torture. Suicidal ideation is common during depressive periods.

Bipolar Disorder is characterized by the presence of both manic and depressive phases, sometimes back-to-back. This mental ping pong negatively affects the lives of those who suffer from the Disorder. The severity and length of time between moods vary; sufferers have the potential to lose their grasp on reality, making the Disorder challenging for the affected person and those who provide care.

Manic Episode

Mania can be characterized by the surplus of energy that an affected individual experiences. The sufferer may feel as though they are strapped into a rollercoaster with no control over their fate. The episodes may come on with no warning, suddenly changing everything.

A manic individual's thoughts are racing, nonstop. They may lay in bed, wide-awake, wishing for rest as their brain is planning new projects and making ill-advised plans. Imagine the exhaustion of not being able to rest for weeks at a time correctly. Sleeping medication is often not powerful enough to dull the symptoms of mania.

Many sufferers are actively taking medication to prevent their transitions into extreme moods, but these medications don't work 100-percent of the time. People who have Bipolar Disorder live with the possibility that they could slip into a manic episode at any time.

Imagine mixing constant stress with the paranoia that comes preloaded into manic episodes. Imagine trying to hold your life together as you watch your own mind slipping away from your control. The familiar symptoms are all creeping back, and you have no choice except to brace for the worst.

Food loses all appeal. Your body is telling your brain that you need no nourishment. Ingesting needed sustenance is tainted with feelings of revulsion.

The ideas seem to flow eternally during manic episodes. The sufferer is plagued with thoughts of productivity and new projects. In the moment, these pursuits feel justified and revolutionary. After the fact, the individual with BP is faced with the harsh reality that so many of their thoughts were delusional.

Every single task feels urgent. The energy feels like a curse because the sufferer is only one individual and cannot complete such a plethora of assignments at once. Mania can cause the feeling that one is too productive to actually produce; there are too many paralyzing entries on the list.

There is also a terrifying aspect of the mania that must be discussed. Sufferers often lose their grasp of reality, becoming swept away in delusions of grandeur. One individual might believe that she is meant to save the world or that she has insights no one else possesses.

Sufferers tend to make uncharacteristic decisions during manic episodes. BP patients may find themselves on massive spending sprees. Other manic individuals may try narcotics or might engage in risky or promiscuous behavior (like cheating on a spouse). Impulsive indulgences rule all aspects of life during these phases.

Depressive Episode

Depressive is very much the opposite of manic in every way. Energy tends to fall to dire levels, leaving the individual feeling hopeless and unable to accomplish anything. Getting out of bed is a significant triumph during a depressive episode.

Negative self-talk causes sufferers to feel as if they are worthless, the polar opposite of manic delusions of grandeur. Individuals may lose or gain large amounts of weight due to appetite fluctuation. Sluggish, forlorn, and dreary, affected people to lose their enthusiasm for daily life as their energy circles the drain.

None of the sufferer's previously loved hobbies bring joy. It can feel as though all of the colors have been sucked from the individual's life. Everything that used to matter is now submerged in a thick layer of fog.

When It Is Not Bipolar Disorder

Before we discuss the symptoms of Bipolar, we must take a look at what is **not** BP. Preexisting medical conditions can make the water murky, making a clear-cut diagnosis more difficult. If you believe that you or a loved one could potentially be living with Bipolar, it can be a good idea to consider other possibilities before seeking treatment.

When discerning if an individual has Bipolar Disorder, there are a few factors that must be considered. People can potentially go through manic and depressive episodes due to catalysts outside of their own cognition. Imagine a woman who finds herself on a cocaine bender; she would present many of the negative symptoms of mania without actually having BP.

A man who is withdrawing from long-term opiate use is going to feel sluggish. The recovering individual will be hopeless and unenthusiastic; his energy levels will absolutely bottom out. If he were to be analyzed by a psychologist with no knowledge of his narcotic use, it might seem as though the man is depressed; he could appear to be having a depressive episode related to Bipolar Disorder.

Various diseases and unrelated medical conditions may also trigger symptoms in patients that mirror the symptoms of Bipolar Disorder. Individuals with Lupus might find themselves feeling sluggish or fatigued. Thyroid issues can cause appetite and weight fluctuations. Underlying medical conditions must be ruled out before a BP diagnosis can be made.

Disorders within the Schizophrenia family may also appear to be Bipolar Disorder, from the right angle. Manic and depressive episodes sometimes feature hallucinations and delusions related to the individual's mood and environment. Schizophrenia causes the same symptoms, but they are independent of stimuli in the patient's own feelings (or mood-incongruent).

Emotional trauma can also cause temporary changes to an individual's psychology and decision-making abilities. Dealing with a significant life-change or the loss of a loved one may bring about depression. These factors can be tricky to navigate because devastating events can also trigger a manic or depressive episode in a person with undiagnosed Bipolar Disorder.

Symptoms of Bipolar Disorder

Bipolar Disorder can be a difficult illness to diagnose because there are so many other conditions that appear similar. Depression and mania also manifest as two completely different and opposite entities, with BP hiding in the details of both. The following section will cover symptoms related to the different extremes.

Mania

- Relationship with sleep changes as rest feels unnecessary for continued function. Individuals with Bipolar Disorder report being able to sleep extraordinarily little while still feeling rested.

- Hallucinations.

- Decision-making abilities change. Throughout manic episodes, people with BP become **impulsive**.

Individuals act with little to no regard for consequences, negatively impacting their lives. Spending massive amounts of money, gambling, narcotics, infidelity, and other indulgences are no longer off-limits.

- Delusions of grandeur cause people to take on responsibilities beyond their skillset. This may take the form of an individual opening a business with no previous experience, no school, and little research. Delusions of grandeur could also see a person believing that they are solely responsible for preventing an oncoming disaster about which no one else knows.

- Restlessness and the feeling that one must continuously engage in activities is a mania symptom.

- Speaking very quickly while stumbling over words and mixing phrases can be a sign of mania. The volume of voice may also appear to increase.

- Fidgeting, pacing, etc.,

- Thoughts seem to race, especially during the night. This is also called the flight of ideas.

- The inability to complete tasks due to distractibility and excitability is also a symptom.

- Sense of euphoria and high self-confidence that lasts for an unusually long time.

Hypomania

Hypomania is a state that exists in-between normal function and mania. An individual in a hypomanic episode still experiences an excitable and prolonged high that can often be mistaken for a sunny disposition. The condition is not so severe as to cause hallucinations, and the sufferer can maintain their grasp on reality.

Hypomania can still potentially damage the lives of those who experience it, as it has a more insidious and discrete influence. Decision making is affected by a euphoric state, which might still lead to reckless behavior, but it is not so intense that others notice. This in-between high also has a tendency to slip into either depression or actual mania.

Depression

- Sleep changes again, this time requiring more and yet, never feeling rested. Intense feelings of fatigue characterize the days of individuals in a depressive state.

- Isolating oneself from loved ones and other people, in general, can indicate depression, and sufferers may try to never leave the safety of their own home.

- Short-term memory becomes fuzzy and unreliable.

- Suicidal ideation and feelings of despondency and hopelessness are also signs of depression.

- Individuals feel low for extended amounts of time with no energy or enthusiasm.

- Over-eating or under-eating may cause changes in weight and health.

- Unable to concentrate or focus. These individuals cannot bring themselves to complete tasks, leading to feelings of guilt.

- Issues with making decisions.

- Loss of enthusiasm for activities that used to be pleasurable (making art, music, a particular sport, learning, reading, anything else that requires energy to engage) can indicate depression.

Mixed Episode

Mixed episodes occur when the individual experiences symptoms of both mania and depression at the same time. It is possible for the high and the low to exist in tandem with one another, producing some unfortunate outcomes. There is a famously grim example associated with the mixture:

Individuals in the throes of a depressive episode often have suicidal ideation. Sometimes the only thing keeping these people alive is their lack of resolve to follow through with their wishes. A mixed state might lend enough energy to prove to be harmful in such situations.

Mixed states are frightening because they carry such a high risk for self-harm or suicide. Irritability, agitation, restlessness, boredom, stress, and anxiety are also common when one is stuck in-between the two extremes. Sufferers may feel as if they are being pulled in two very different directions by their own minds.

Types of Bipolar Disorder

Unfortunately, Bipolar Disorder does not have one playbook that operates across every individual with the illness. BP is as nuanced as the individuals who suffer from it, causing even more diagnostic confusion. The following breaks down the three types you need to know:

Bipolar I
Bipolar I is the most renowned form of the Disorder. An individual with BP I experiences episodes that involve **mania**,

either pure or in a mixed state. In most cases, the individual has experiences depressive states.

Bipolar II

BP II sufferers do not experience full mania. These individuals cycle between hypomania and intense **depressive** episodes. It can be much easier to live with this form of the illness, but damage will likely still be caused to one's life as a result of the phases. Friendships, relationships, and work-life may suffer as a result of BP-II.

Those who experience hypomania are unlikely to report remembering the affected time as being anything other than usual.

Cyclothymia

This is a variation that seeks to characterize a lesser form of BP. Sufferers are familiar with hypomania and often slip into a mild state of depression. The lack of intensity means that many of these individuals remain undiagnosed.

Bipolar NOS

NOS means "Not Otherwise Specified." This iteration of the Disorder is characterized by episodes of hypomania only. When an individual does not experience depressive episodes and only mild mania, they may be diagnosed with NOS.

Other Variations

The diagnosis of BP has expanded to include patients who have acquired the Disorder through drug use or in relation to a separate medical condition.

Diagnostics

The process for receiving a diagnosis for Bipolar Disorder will involve seeking the attention of a mental health professional (psychologist or psychiatrist). Either through a questionnaire or verbal interview, the patient will be asked about their family's history with mental illness. BP has a genetic component that can be compared to other lifestyle factors. The professional will also ask questions to rule out factors like drug use or loss that may falsely present as BP.

Relevant questions center around energy levels, lifestyle, drug use, and experience with mania and depression. The minimum requirements for a Bipolar diagnosis include one episode of mania or hypomania and one episode of depression. Manic states must last for at least one week. Manic episodes must also have three of the symptoms from the list mentioned previously. Depression must endure for at least two weeks and include four of the symptoms, as discussed above. To be diagnosed with **Cyclothymia** (the mild form of BP), symptoms must have already existed for two years for adults.

When an illness is labeled "disorder," it tends to mean that it has negatively affected the lives of those diagnosed. The psychologist will ask questions about the way symptoms have impacted the patient's life and the level of control the person maintained over their actions. Friends and family may also be useful references during this process, as people are often too biased to self-report.

The psychologist will also seek to identify **rapid cycling**, should the patient have Bipolar Disorder. Rapid cycling is a form of the illness that inflicts four episodes upon the individual, during the course of a year. When mental illness is left untreated, it has the potential to develop into a more sinister and damaging variation of itself.

Chapter 2: Treatment and Assistance

Individuals who suffer from Bipolar Disorder lament that they despise depressive episodes, but a good portion find themselves wistfully romanticizing the manic highs. This can make treatment complicated as the medication takes away both extremes, making patients less likely to commit to their regimen. Giving up productive euphoria in exchange for a less cumbersome existence can be difficult.

There is a difference between mania and happiness, as the latter is not particularly harmful. Individuals who have found legitimate joy in their lives don't overindulge in risky or damaging behaviors. Doctors are tasked with being able to spot these discrepancies, though most patients will only seek treatment during the depressive portion of their illness.

Statistics concerning the treatment of BP are not inspiring. Only twenty percent of individuals who test positive for the illness in some way are ever actually given the diagnosis. Thirty-one percent walk away with a diagnosis of depression. The remainder is not diagnosed at all.

Of the twenty percent that were correctly diagnosed, most were just given an anti-depressant with no mood stabilizer. The before-mentioned treatment is not the standard of care for individuals suffering from BP. When dealing with an illness that has such a high mortality rate (through suicide), it is imperative that care matches severity.

Up to twenty-five percent of those with Bipolar Disorder who remain untreated will attempt suicide. Men are usually more successful with the action, which makes being male a risk factor for premature death.

Treatment Through Medication

Medication is a hotly debated topic for illnesses like BP. When an aspect of the Disorder makes the sufferer feel as though they can conquer the world, drugs that dull the senses can be undesirable. Throughout this book, we will detail a number of options so that the reader will feel more informed about different available pathways to wellness.

Lithium Salts

Lithium is the most famous and most popular medication for the treatment of Bipolar Disorder. There is no risk for substance abuse because the drug has no euphoric or physiological effects in healthy individuals. Some antipsychotic and anti-epileptic medicine can increase the effectiveness of lithium salts even more.

Lithium has been proven to work well with mania, causing an improvement in sixty to eighty percent of cases it is used to treat. The compound was initially meant to offer a salt alternative to the masses, first appearing in the forties. Toxicity wiped the product from the shelves; it can be damaging to consume in the wrong dosages.

Side-effects make the medication a risky choice, but it is the most effective drug in treatment, as of now. Intense monitoring is needed to ensure that individuals prescribed lithium are not displaying any adverse effects. Psychologists must be vigilant to protect the physical and mental health of their patients, working around a narrow therapeutic threshold (too little does nothing and too much will make a person sick).

Lithium is monitored through blood levels. The drug does not breakdown in the system; instead, it is excreted as waste, or the patient sweats it out. The medication becomes stable in the body after about two weeks of consumption.

Unfortunately, lithium can be dangerous. The success of the treatment must be weighed against the potential damage it might cause. Because the substance is not metabolized in the body but instead runs through the kidneys, any action or medication that changes kidney function could also throw-off lithium levels. The following is a list of the dangers associated with this treatment option:

- Short-term memory may experience a decline in functionality.
- Issues with digestion and nausea.
- Issues with cognition.
- Fluctuations in urination.
- Weight gain.
- General toxicity when the renal balance is thrown-off is another side-effect. The smallest change to kidney function could be dangerous for a patient taking lithium.

Mood Stabilizers

Mood stabilizers were created to be used as anti-convulsant. The family of medications has also had success with pain relief, treating drug and alcohol succession (withdraw tremors), and regulating mood.

Carbamazepine works as well as lithium salts, with regard to treating mania and its reoccurrence. This medication also carries the potential for issues with cognition. The drug also has the potential for a strangely deadly skin condition that favors Asian populations.

Valproic Acid works partially through suppressing neural firing and has been used to treat rapid cycling Bipolar Disorder and mania (in addition to schizoaffective Disorder). The side effects include a sedation haze, stomach upset, hair loss, and tremors.

Lamotrigine has been found to offer a high level of success when treating Bipolar Disorder I. Instead of decreasing cognition, this medication has actually been shown to improve cognitive function. One of the most undesirable outcomes of taking medicines for BP is the zombie-like haze that is inflicted upon patients, and Lamotrigine solves that issue.

These are just some of the most notable medications in the mood stabilizer family that have been shown to treat Bipolar Disorder. These medications also help with anxiety, PTSD, alcohol withdrawal, and aggression. Finding the correct drug may involve trial and error, but it can be essential to consider the side-effects as well as the benefits (especially with substances like valproic acid).

Atypical Antipsychotics

Second-generation antipsychotics have been used to successfully treat the manic episodes that present themselves in Bipolar Disorder. *Risperidone* helps sustain remission. *Olanzapine* aids with depressive episodes.

Quetiapine has been shown to improve BP in the areas of mania, depression, and maintenance. Recent studies on a drug called *lurasidone* have also displayed promising results. The medication also typically manifests an improvement within two weeks of patient consumption; anxiety and quality of life also typically change for the better.

Omega-3 Fatty Acid

There has been experimental research conducted to evaluate the role of omega-3 in fighting Bipolar Disorder, with promising results. In countries that typically consume a high-fish diet, there are noticeably fewer instances of BP among the population. Preliminary studies have shown that patients improved their symptoms through increasing their omega-3 intake, without taking any additional medication.

Common medical knowledge already associates omega-3 fatty acids with the health of the human brain. There are no damaging side-effects, so adding fish to a treatment plan could only benefit the individual, even if early results are still inconclusive. Dietary changes have the potential to be a fruitful field of study in association with the treatment of BP.

Treatments of Bipolar Disorder should consider the effectiveness of the therapy, the safety of the patient, convenience, and the individual's ability/willingness to continue with the treatment modality. The aim of treatment should be to eliminate depression, and ideally to maintain a stable mood.

People with BP often find themselves prescribed several medications at one time. Drugs like *lurasidone*-that do not interact poorly with other substances are ideal for this type of treatment. Doctors will still monitor closely for adverse effects.

Going Off the Meds

Individuals with Bipolar Disorder often find themselves struggling with medication. Mania can be euphoric, which causes even more distress when patients feel as though they are sedated. The side-effects must be considered so that both psychologists and patients can create an open line of communication. No one is going to stick to a treatment that does not work for them.

There are several reasons why sufferers ditch their medication. Studies have concluded that somewhere between seventy and ninety percent of BP patients have stopped taking their prescriptions at some point during their treatment. This happens mostly with people who are new to the diagnosis. Why?

The Medication Works: Occasionally, the efficacy of the medication can work against patients, especially if they are questioning the diagnosis. It can seem as if the issues have simply disappeared when a patient finds the right combination of drugs. Enthusiastic sufferers decide that a mistake has been made, and they let go of their entire treatment plan.

If you know someone who has taken a hard left away from their treatment, or if you have done so yourself, know that it isn't a fatal mistake. According to the statistics, forsaking your plan is almost bound to happen at some point. Part of treating this disorder often involves venturing off the path and then back on again.

Loved ones of people who have stopped taking their medication may find themselves feeling like giving up. Investing effort into helping someone who doesn't seem to want the help can be exhausting. Understand that these emotions are absolutely valid. Bipolar Disorder is a scary diagnosis, and it can be a difficult thing for people to come to terms with. Finding the right treatment plan is going to be a massive part of the process. Leaving the path, occasionally, is going to be an absolutely regular occurrence.

Side-effects: There is a stigma associated with the medication prescribed to people with Bipolar Disorder, and there is a reason for the stigma. Some of the drugs that doctors prescribe have intense effects on cognition and may even make the individual feel sedated. Weight gain and diminished libido can also harm a person's general quality of life.

There is no reason for a patient to continue along a path that seems to be causing more harm than good. Finding a psychologist that specializes in mood disorders (or Bipolar Disorder, specifically) is a great first step toward fixing this issue. Options exist for those who respond negatively to certain drugs.

Do not give up on all medication because of one bad experience. The right combination exists for everyone. Medicine is constantly evolving and can vastly improve the quality of life for so many people.

Funding: Medication for Bipolar Disorder is not cheap. Sometimes there is a lack of cash flow, and that prevents patients from being able to purchase vital medication. Luckily, there are options out there for struggling sufferers. Assistance programs in different locations exist.

Find the manufacturer of your specific medication and use a search engine to find their patient assistance program. These resources are typically unknown and unutilized.

Vanishing Personality: Sufferers often worry that through taking medication they will lose the part of themselves that they love. Sedation and zombie-like-haze characterize this fear. When patients respond poorly to a medication, it can often be because the dosage is too high.

Worries like these are another reason to find a specialist and maintain an open dialogue. Fixing sedation could be as easy as micro-dosing or knocking a few hundred milligrams off your daily regimen. The fear of becoming dull and losing cognition is not unfounded; the portrayal of BP treatment in popular culture has been bleak. Know that you are not trapped in any one medication plan. If something is not working, be sure to consult your doctor and share how you feel.

Inability to See Sickness: Bipolar Disorder can change perception dramatically. Sufferers, especially ones in the throes of a manic episode, may not see anything wrong with themselves. Friends and loved ones are likely to realize that the patient is still suffering, but the patient may have no clue.

Dependence: Sufferers are often afraid to become dependent on medication for the rest of their lives. Bipolar Disorder is a severe illness that is treated with the seriousness that it deserves. Culture has attached a strange stigma to needing medication for psychological anomalies.

Any person with a physical ailment has no issue regarding their medication as a necessary part of their life. BP should be viewed through the same lens. Should you suffer from the illness, do not let the ignorant change the way that you view your medication. It has as much importance as heart attack medication, and it's OK to take it every day.

Shame: Our treatment of the mentally ill has come a long way since the days of lobotomies and involuntary shock therapy, but that does not mean that we are perfect yet. There is still work to be done with regard to the way psychological disorders are viewed within society. Some individuals with BP become ashamed of the medication that they take, resulting in them not following their treatment protocol.

Friends and loved ones can change a patient's life by supporting and protecting the sufferer. BP causes vulnerability and confusion in otherwise brilliant individuals. Those who suffer from this Disorder need their loved ones to stand by; they need an influence that is louder than the rest of the world.

Therapy for Bipolar Disorder

Medication is only one element of treatment for individuals with Bipolar Disorder. Psychologists and psychiatrists often offer Therapy in addition to a prescription plan. Individuals suffering from BP need a custom path to wellness that addresses their unique symptoms, and usually this involves a combination of modalities.

Cognitive Behavioral Therapy

Cognitive Behavioral Therapy, or CBT, is one of the most common treatments recommended to people who have been diagnosed with Bipolar Disorder. Medication is the first line of defense, but psychologists have been studying the addition of CBT to an existing plan of action with promising results.

Studies from UCLA posit that Cognitive Behavioral Therapy in tandem with medication, has been shown to reduce the number of episodes in patients. Extreme moods are shorter and often less intense. Family therapy has also been shown to aid in the easing of symptoms.

Cognitive Behavioral Therapy can teach patients to identify the early warning signs that an episode could be on the horizon. Through understand what precedes a cycle, individuals gain the ability to notice patterns in their thinking and actions in relation to depression or mania. Through controlling their own psychology, people can alter their state of mind.

These early signs can also be used to brace for the storm in ways that change the severity of the episode. If an individual feels as though they might be headed toward a depression, they would seek to stay away from elements that intensify negative feelings. Patients can use their new knowledge in the same way that we might use a weather forecast.

Cognitive Behavioral Therapy also educates patients about the importance of sleep and the influence of the circadian rhythm on mood. Individuals with BP have been shown to have a sensitivity to changes in their cycle, especially when compared to people without the illness. The affected person will be wise to plan and coordinate their schedule. Strict commitment to the itinerary will allow for stability and may help to regulate emotions.

Family therapy may be included alongside the CBT to ensure that the patient's loved ones are on the look-out for the same warning signs. The immediate circle may also be useful for ensuring that the individual with Bipolar Disorder adheres to the schedule that they have created for themselves; accountability can extend out beyond the therapist's office. In general, it can be a good idea to foster the creation of a support system for the patient.

Family-Focused Therapy

Family-Focused Therapy (FFT) is also a popular treatment for individuals with Bipolar Disorder. The family and loved ones of those with the diagnosis are taught what it means to have BP, and the symptoms and signs that could indicate trouble ahead. The patient's closest circle is encouraged to develop a plan of action to stop relapses before they start.

The point of Family-Focused Therapy is to establish the family as a support system. A mental health professional will guide members of the group through their built-up resentment and tension. The patient and their loved ones leave this treatment feeling like a team.

Family-Focused Therapy is still in its early stages of development but has been shown to improve the lives of those involved. When compared to other existing treatments (like CBT), the program performed just as well.

Interpersonal and Social Rhythm Therapy

Interpersonal and Social Rhythm Therapy (or IPSRT) was developed to educate individuals with a Bipolar diagnosis, to aid in a better understanding of the illness. IPSRT also serves to teach affected patients to pinpoint and learn to modify behaviors associated with mood swings. Variations of the program have even been created to delay symptoms in adolescents with a strong likelihood of having BP.

As the name suggests, IPSRT also examines the role of the circadian rhythm in a patient's life. People who suffer from Bipolar Disorder are much more sensitive to changes within their schedule. So many of the symptoms of BP center around this cycle, from insomnia to changes in appetite.

Some psychologists believe that the symptoms of Bipolar Disorder are mangled portions of the circadian rhythm. IPSRT posits that regularity in the schedule will change the onset of symptoms of BP. One of the most important aspects of a patient's life should be stability.

Patients are held accountable for keeping a regular schedule. Every fundamental activity should be maintained and practiced at the same time, daily. Food and sleep should be monitored with a commitment to the plan.

Patients are not able to control the time they're able to fall asleep, but they can control the amount of rest they allow their body to achieve. Individuals with BP are asked to keep a mood tracker that measures the stability of their day to the evenness of their emotions. Psychologists are finding that there are strong correlations between schedule and temperament.

Chapter 3: Alternative Treatments

In the previous chapter, we took a look at the most popular medications and therapies for individuals with Bipolar Disorder. The treatments mentioned so far are only a small portion of the options available to patients with a BP diagnosis. This section will take a broader look at other paths that might be taken on the journey to wellness.

Bright Light Therapy

Bright Light Therapy was developed to help individuals with symptoms of Seasonal Affective Disorder (SAD). People suffering from SAD find themselves depressed during the dark winter months, only to find relief in the spring and summer. Studies on Bright Light Therapy initially showed promising results for the improvement of seasonally depressed patients.

The research was then expanded to include Unipolar Depression and then Bipolar Disorder. The study consisted of shining a bright bulb at patients with a BP diagnosis for fifteen minutes a day. The scientists gradually increased the number of time participants spent in front of the blub, to a full hour. By week six, almost seventy percent of the participants noticed a remission of their symptoms.

However, participants in the study were also placed on mood stabilizers for the duration of the project, skewing the results some. Researchers were worried that the Therapy might trigger a manic episode without the addition of the medication. This is a new treatment, but the research is promising so far, especially considering our knowledge of the way circadian rhythms deeply affect those with BP.

During the experiment, when Light Therapy was given in the morning, patients began to experience hypomania. The researchers moved the Therapy to the afternoon, and this is when they received the positive results.

Botulinum Toxin Injection
One of the most effective ways to stop an overactive fight or flight response is to control your breathing. Controlled breathing tricks the body into thinking that the danger has passed. A signal is sent to the brain to slow the production of stress hormones, and the crisis is averted.

We can learn a lot from the way our body responds to stimuli. The amygdala is connected to your face muscles that react to harmful stimuli and is also responsible for many of our most unpleasant feelings. When you hear bad news, your forehead tenses and your brow furrows in response.

Treating the muscles of the face that tense, frown or furrow, has served to calm the amygdala. Eric Finzi, MD, Ph.D., recently created a study with incredible early results showing that BP can be controlled by using the above treatment. In the study, a handful of patients with Bipolar Disorder were injected with the botulinum toxin, which calms the muscles.

The toxin was placed right inside the brow muscles. All of the participants showed an improvement, with over half experiencing remission of their symptoms. When the toxin wore off, the symptoms returned, suggesting that this would require ongoing injections to be a viable treatment method.

Ketamine

Ketamine has a bit of deserved stigma surrounding it, but lately, it has also been showing beneficial results when it comes to treating people with a Bipolar diagnosis. Trials have shown the drug to improve symptoms for around half of the participants involved. Scientists are only now studying the way ketamine might help those with depression and mood disorders.

One of the most cumbersome aspects of finding a new medication is deciphering all of the side-effects. Weight gain is high up on the list of undesirable reactions. Patients are also worried about sedation and dulled cognitive function.

Additional research needs to be conducted, but thus far Ketamine appears to be a viable modality for treating the symptoms of Bipolar Disorder in some people.

Vitamins

One must be wary of any advice about herbal remedies for Bipolar Disorder. Natural remedies have the potential to assist in the right treatment plan, but so much information available online is based on little to no research. The following vitamins have been proven, through studies, to provide beneficial results for some Bipolar patients:

1. Vitamin B3
2. Vitamin B6
3. Vitamin C

Advice for Herbal Treatments

As mentioned above, it is essential to do homework when researching possible remedies. There are popular supplements like (5-HTP and St John's Wort), but there are also obscure advertisements on the internet offering impossibly simple cures for Bipolar Disorder. Before taking any new supplements, it is vital that you consult with your doctor first to make sure they are safe and won't interact badly with any of your current medication.

Every individual is entitled to seek out precisely the sort of treatment that works for them. Medication and Therapy will provide a baseline of treatment, but herbal supplements can also be of assistance when taken in the right dosages.

Ways to Manage the Illness

We have looked at some innovative new treatments for BP, but there are also measures that an affected person can personally take to help control the illness. The following are tips and tricks that can be used to gain more control over Bipolar Disorder.

Triggers

Through Therapy or on one's own, triggers can be identified. Patients with BP may find that they are stressed out by family tension or work expectations. Irregular sleep is an insanely common trigger that remains consistent among most individuals that suffer from Bipolar Disorder.

Affected people can document their triggers. This will allow for a measure of control over the illness. Triggers can be managed to lessen or eliminate their effects. By understanding what triggers their Bipolar episodes, a person can proactively try to avoid and manage these triggers. This likely won't lead to the cessation of manic or depressive episodes altogether, but it can dramatically reduce their severity and duration.

Mood Journal

Patients are encouraged to keep track of their emotions. Manic and depressive episodes typically present themselves following a pattern of changes. Through careful recordkeeping, one can predict when they are about to slip into an extreme state. Mood journals can also be helpful for monitoring progress.

Eliminate Stimulating Light

Everything that we have learned so far points to individuals with BP being very sensitive to schedule. Science has also shown us that our brains process blue light as sunlight, tricking the circadian rhythm. The illumination from our various electronics has inspired a gigantic wave of insomnia across all age groups, in the developed world.

Individuals suffering from Bipolar Disorder are encouraged to buy glasses or some other form of protection for their eyes at night. When patients find themselves using the phone before bed, they should search for a blue light filter within the settings. People with a Bipolar diagnosis should choose a set time every single day to shut off their electronics.

Scheduling

This point is going to appear over and over again because it is relevant in so many different areas of treatment. When individuals with BP feel as though they are losing control of their lives, solace can be found through the design of, and strict adherence to, a schedule. Patients should set aside time for whatever actives they can predict in advance.

Handling Rage

Bipolar Disorder is not a cut and dry illness. The highs are not always *just* highs, and the lows are equally problematic. Sometimes, sufferers are left feeling a terrible mixture of manic and depressive at the same time. Paranoia, agitation, and rage are the most common emotions associated with this phase.

Mixed states are incredibly dangerous. As mentioned before, these are the times that afflicted individuals are most likely to take their own life—feeling as though you are worthless and finally having the energy to deal with the issue is a horrible combination.

There are a few ways for those with BP to control their mixed states and their rage with more success. Feeling angry for no reason can be one of the most frustrating emotions. Sufferers are often inclined to invent villains, so they have a place to direct their fury.

By learning to accept that there is no logical reason for the anger, the affected person can talk themselves out of smiting others with their wrath. **Self-awareness** is a crucial aspect of dealing with Bipolar Disorder. When the person with Bipolar challenges and trains themselves to be honest about their emotions, their power is regained.

Self-awareness is not a miraculous cure, and the sufferer will likely still feel their anger. The point here is to be conscious of the anger, and to not to direct the rage at an undeserving party. These emotions never last forever, and the Bipolar person has no other responsibility but to hold on until the storm passes.

Manic rage and mixed states need to be addressed when they occur. These are some of the most dangerous and tense moments for both the mentally ill individual and those close to them.

In extreme cases, the unadulterated rage can lead to violence. Undeserved aggression and abuse are just another reason that so many untreated Bipolar people find themselves behind bars. The irritation starts off so small that the sufferer usually doesn't even notice. Negative emotions can continue to build until they break through the surface with a vengeance.

Relationships are destroyed. Jobs are lost. Freedom is taken away. Mixed state anger is a severe symptom and needs to be treated with the importance that it deserves.

A study was conducted that showed one-third of bipolar individuals have mentioned suffering from bouts of uncontrollable rage. These breakdowns are not uncommon, and especially in youth, they should be taken as a sign that an individual is potentially suffering from BP. Substance abuse and caffeine can drastically add to the irritability.

Cutting extraneous substances from one's life can make a world of difference in the life of the sufferer. These substances cause irritability and agitation on their own. Any activity or chemical that serves to change the emotional state of the person who ingests it will affect Bipolar people more; that is just the nature of the illness.

Stop and reflect on the situation. The person with Bipolar can stop themselves for just a moment and assess the way they feel, asking a question like, "If I were happy, would this issue still bother me?" Being honest with oneself is one of the most important tools a person with BP has in their arsenal.

Don't feed the hatred. Feeling rage is strangely addicting to most people. Even though anger is a negative emotion, many people take no issue with entering a tense situation. BP sufferers have the same tendency to add fuel to their own fire. Knowing that an action will cause further agitation and continuing with it anyway is feeding the flame.

One may separate themselves from their anger by taking the opportunity to walk away for a moment. Going into another room is always an option. Exercising out the extra energy may also be helpful. Possessing the ability to excuse yourself from the situation can take a massive amount of motivation and willpower, but it is worth the struggle to deescalate the conflict. The ability to do this will also improve over time.

Mitigate damage by staying away from forms of digital or voice communication. Typing out a furious status or sending a rage-filled text message can be so tempting in the moment. Shame will always follow these exchanges. People say regrettable things when they are furious. When the situation calms back down, feelings completely change.

Control your breathing and find a place where you feel safe. Use this chance to defuse and do not enter a space with others until you can calmly articulate your thoughts. Sufferers should try to remember that the rage is caused by the illness and not by their loved ones.

Emergency Medication can be useful in situations where the sufferer feels as though they might lose control. Something like

Xanax or Valium would slow the progression of thoughts and calm the afflicted person back down to a stable point. Asking a doctor for this medication is just fine, as long as it is only to be used in case of an emergency. These substances are addictive and should only be consumed occasionally. CBT is a beautiful alternative for those who do not wish to take narcotics.

Chapter 4: Brave New World

Highly Functioning

Throughout this entire book, we have learned that Bipolar Disorder is not a one-size-fits-all illness. BP is a severe diagnosis, but some forms present with more mild symptoms, like the less intense hypomania. Functionality is not congruent with struggle, though, and every separate individual carries their burden differently.

The word stigma has been mentioned a lot and is brought up often when discussing mental illness. Bipolar Disorder is not safe from the stereotyping eyes of the masses, no matter how flattering or offensive the assumptions may be.

Some of the most accomplished creative minds in human history have lived with Bipolar Disorder. Vincent Van Gogh, Jimi Hendrix, Virginia Woolf, and even Ernest Hemingway can all be counted among those who weathered the intense highs and lows of BP. A sizeable list of contemporary actors, musicians, and artists have detailed their battles with Bipolar.

So many people who suffer from Bipolar Disorder seem to find success in career fields that require abstract thought and interpretation, but what about everyone else? Are there Bipolar math teachers, accountants, doctors, or lawyers? Are there sufferers who can hold down nine-to-five jobs throughout their darkest days? In short, yes.

Some people with Bipolar Disorder will never share their diagnosis, and no one around them will be able to tell. The conversation surrounding functionality does not end with less intense types of the illness (like Cyclothymia). Some individuals can manage themselves and their symptoms so effectively that people often are unaware of their Bipolar diagnosis to begin with.

"Highly functioning" is not always a choice; sometimes, it is about survival. The term means that the illness does not hinder the person's interaction with the world around them, and they can maintain their career or their education. Bad days are handled with an impressive amount of grace because moving forward is the only option.

Many professionals with a Bipolar diagnosis will never share that information with their coworkers or employers; these people suffer in silence, fearing that those two words would change the fundamental nature of their relationship with clients and peers. BP sufferers often worry that they cannot be taken seriously or that they will no longer be trusted in the workplace.

If you do not have the illness, imagine for a moment that you do. Imagine that people at your place of employment have somehow discovered this information. Every single time you laugh, you now have to worry that your peers believe you are in the throes of an episode. Genuine displays of emotion could be held beneath a microscope, mainly because the average person lacks knowledge on what having Bipolar Disorder really entails.

Keeping the diagnosis to yourself is also a challenge of astronomical proportions. Imagine adjusting to the strange side-effects of new medication while you are also trying to complete an important project at work. Imagine waking up with lead in your limbs and feeling as though the world is caving in upon you, then having to force yourself to get to work or school on time while keeping a straight face.

Highly functioning individuals face difficulties that others will struggle to understand. Keeping a mental illness secret through camouflage or a thick façade is isolating.

Maintaining a normal life through the intense ups and downs does not mean that these individuals have a milder form of BP; it only means that they have found ways to cope with their symptoms. Many highly functioning people have simply decided to devote all of their energy to the cause, diverting potential breakdowns until they are alone.

Losing control can often be the difference between living in a comfortable home or on the streets/behind bars. Statistics show that seventy-two percent of BP sufferers have had run-ins with substance abuse. Manic episodes also increase the possibility of incarceration.

Bipolar Disorder does not drastically affect intelligence or academic ability, which presents a unique set of challenges for those living with the illness. Patients are more likely to lose assets because they can gain them in the first place. An unfortunate connection also exists between BP and housing instability.

Individuals who can maintain their lifestyle can feel as though they are suspended from a thin thread, above an open flame. The consequences of letting go during a manic or depressive episode can be catastrophic. Each obstacle must be approached with an extreme amount of energy, leaving the sufferers able to do little more than making it through their work or school day.

Scientific evidence has suggested that having close interpersonal connections is also imperative for the mental health of Bipolar patients. Having a support system made of friends and family with whom the sufferer can vent frustrations lessens the overall expression of the illness. Having trusted social bonds means fewer episodes.

So many high-functioning people keep their diagnosis private to their own detriment, preventing them from creating the support system that would help with navigation of the illness. The isolating nature of BP is another cruel aspect that serves to further complicate the lives of those who suffer. A delicate balance must be struck to live an ideal version of a life with Bipolar Disorder. Choosing to prioritize work leaves little room for anything else. Choosing to fall to the whims of extreme moods often lands patients in legal or financial distress.

High functionality can also be the product of a treatment plan that is doing its job. There is a difference between healthy and harmful coping. Not every Bipolar person who excels in their career field is suffering at home. With the help of medical professionals, patients can learn to live a (mostly) normal life.

Reflection is necessary to determine the nature of success for highly functional people with BP. Doing well is either the product of appropriately balancing your life or wearing a thick mask that no one else can see through. It is imperative to seek treatment for the illness, even if a patient's symptoms appear to be managed well.

Individuals who excel within their career paths may feel as though they are not obligated to attend Therapy because they seem to be doing alright on their own. Treatment is always a net positive, and it can help with facilitating the need for a support network. Bipolar Disorder comes with a wealth of intense emotions and moods that must be expressed. The bottling up of one's stresses only adds to the pile.

Work and Bipolar Disorder

Less than three percent of all adults have Bipolar Disorder, and around half are unemployed. Depressive episodes mean that it can be difficult for affected people to even get out of bed. Dragging oneself to the office can seem impossible during these intense mood changes.

Almost ninety percent of Bipolar people with steady jobs maintain that the condition affects the way they handle their work. Major depressive episodes are not the only challenge to overcome. Short-term memory loss and issues with focusing can wreak havoc on a BP mind during the best of days.

Mania has its own disadvantages, but in an occupational environment, it can actually be somewhat beneficial. BP sufferers have the energy and creativity to pursue innovative ideas during these euphoric episodes. Charm seems to explode through the roof, and these individuals can convince bosses and coworkers that they can see work-related projects to fruition. Bipolar patients in sales positions may especially find themselves excelling as they navigate the highs of their illness.

Risk-taking behaviors can be a gamble depending on the occupation, and in this way, mania presents issues. When those with BP are up, they are overconfident and overzealous. Assuming too much responsibility, too much work, and overscheduling can all be issues associated with the extra energy.

Going to work while managing BP can be trying. During depressive phases, when confidence is at an all-time low, it can feel as though the sufferer is an imposter. Therapy and the right support system can make all the difference in reminding the patient that they are more than able to pull through the lows and are the same person that they have always been.

Disclosing Bipolar at Work

According to the ADA (Americans with Disabilities Act), a person with a mental illness is not required to disclose the diagnosis to their employer during the hiring process. Those affected by disorders are not required to share the information at all until they need time away, or accommodation for their condition. It is vital to research and reference the ADA when confused about what information must be shared with employers or associates.

Deciding to disclose BP to others in a professional environment can be a tasking decision for all of the reasons mentioned at the beginning of this chapter. Sometimes, letting others know can be a relief, especially if they have a solid understanding of the illness and what it entails. Unfortunately, most people are uninformed, which makes the conversation a risky endeavor.

When an individual suffering from BP is working for an informed business, revealing themselves can be a positive experience. Patients are often going to behave in ways that others might find strange; adding important context to actions that otherwise may have seemed peculiar. Sympathy can also be valuable in a professional setting. Imagine that the employee is required to dash away to their doctor's appointments frequently; their superior's knowledge of the situation could be a safeguard for repercussions.

Disclosing a diagnosis at a less informed place of employment can lead to coworkers treating the affected individual as if they are fragile. Having projects taken off of your hands because your boss sees you as a liability can be very frustrating.

If Bipolar Disorder is causing performance issues for the diagnosed individual, it can be worthwhile to share the information with an employer. The human resources department exists for situations like these and can ensure that the appropriate parties are informed without turning the disclosure into news or gossip for the entire workplace. Exceptions could potentially be made to accommodate the affected person before any undeserved consequences are enforced.

Occasionally, when accommodations are made, the employer could require a doctor's note for proof of ailment. The letter also does not have to include the name of the illness; it must only state that there is a disability. How much or how little information is shared comes down to the preference of the affected individual.

Accommodations might take the form of a more flexible schedule or a private workspace. Associates should be careful not to request anything outlandish. Every business should have an accommodation policy, and it might be beneficial to consult the literature before taking the position.

Those with Bipolar Disorder are often better served by waiting until they are established at the business, especially if they only plan on sharing the information with their boss or their peers. Making the disclosure as soon as an individual is hired can make the mental illness a permanent first impression.

Should a leave of absence ever become necessary, it can be a good idea to open a line of communication between the individual with Bipolar Disorder and the human resources department at their place of employment. If the associate finds themselves incapacitated, a loved one could take on the role of informing the employer. A plan of action should be set in place beforehand, so the individual with BP and their support system are ready if a hospital stay is imminent.

Returning from a leave of absence should be incremental until the ill party is well enough to return to their former responsibilities; having this option is another reason to maintain open communication throughout the departure. Integrating affected associates back into their former workspace should be made as comfortable as possible.

Finding the Right Job

For some people diagnosed with Bipolar, the prospect of finding and keeping a job is impossible. The illness exists on a spectrum, and individuals who experience intense depressive episodes, hallucinations, and delusions cannot enter the workforce. Every single person must walk the path that is right for them; being incapacitated by such an extreme disorder is not a choice.

Having a passion and a purpose can help with the lows, while utilizing the energy of the highs. Those who are able would benefit from finding the right job, or at least a hobby to occupy their time. How should a diagnosed person go about securing a position that would help them instead of antagonizing the illness?

The first step should include introspection. Everyone has a skill or a passion that could potentially be made into a career. Job hunters who are unsure of their abilities should bring the question up during a therapy session for insight into discovering their ideal vocation.

Evaluating aptitudes and limitations is another essential part of finding a job. Some people are good at clerical work while others are better working with their hands. Some people cannot stand for long periods, and others can't focus on administrative duties.

Passions, strengths, and weaknesses should all be taken into account when trying to discern the correct career path. There are plenty of online job placement tests that could offer inspiration to the searching party. Figuring out the future is like sorting a complex puzzle with lots of different pieces; the Bipolar individual must find a way to make the image come together.

Trying out different jobs can also be an effective way to discover what works for the individual. Smaller, part-time positions have their benefits and may help to provide a sense of purpose, even when they don't serve to express a passion. Having a reason to get out of bed is the only thing that pulls some people from beneath the sheets, especially during a depressive episode.

Having a job also provides structure to those with BP, which is especially imperative as their emotional state can feel chaotic. So much of a diagnosed person's life becomes all about the Disorder and how to handle their intense moods. Employment can also offer a way to escape the grid; affected individuals are offered a chance to forget about their obstacles for a while.

The self-esteem of Bipolar people takes a hit during depressive episodes, but employment offers a chance to improve feelings of self-worth. Having a tangible task to complete can be pleasant for those who spend much of their time battling a gigantic abstract force. Jobs are also a fantastic way to indulge in small amounts of human contact, and potentially even make new friends.

The apparent benefits of employment include making money and living a more active life. Therapy and treatment are not cheap, especially without insurance. Working can drastically improve the quality of life in so many ways when the individual is capable of maintaining a job.

People suffering from Bipolar Disorder often have to navigate gaps in their job history. Volunteering or taking easy classes can be an excellent way to fill those blanks. All charity and educational activities should be listed on the resume in service of "prepping for the next position."

Individuals suffering from BP are sometimes fearful of committing themselves to one place from nine in the morning to five p.m. five days a week. Staying stationary for so long dramatically increases the chances that the affected person will have to work during an episode. Fortunately, there are so many more alternative options to explore.

Work from home positions is becoming more and more prevalent. Seasonal employment is also an option for those that worry about being trapped in a job for too long. Contract work is always available online. Flexible part-time positions are perfect for those who need to be able to manipulate their schedule. Part of finding the right career is deciding what sort of arrangement would best fit.

Research can help to determine the specifics of potential jobs, which might narrow the search down. Deciding on the best match requires the prospect to find out about work responsibilities, compensation, benefits, the opportunity for advancement, hours, conditions, and the required education. Most employers will have this information freely available on job search sites. Websites that review the performance of the potential employer might also be a useful tool.

Public services (known as Vocational Rehabilitation) also exist that are specifically meant to help those with disabilities find adequate employment. The nearest office to you can be located through searching online. Bipolar individuals who are looking to break into the workforce but are unsure of where to start can find assistance through these programs.

Vocational Rehabilitation can help clients meet the required education for a prospective employment position, sometimes even volunteering financial aid. The public service can also help with career evaluations, job counseling, resume building, and job hunting. Resources exist for those who are interested in finding a new purpose.

Chapter 5: Age and Gender

What does early detection look like for Bipolar? With such a high mortality rate, does early detection help those who suffer from the illness? How exactly is Bipolar Disorder spotted in younger children?

Early Detection

Most Bipolar Individuals have their first episode before the age of twenty. Psychologists have stated that young ladies usually have their first primary depressive phase around the same time they hit puberty. Watching for the early warning signs that the illness is on its way can make a surprising difference to long-term health outcomes.

Early detection is very beneficial, but it's also extremely difficult. Individuals with Bipolar Disorder are disproportionately likely to use drugs. Now consider that a manic episode is usually the first indicator to psychiatrists that the individual is ill with something that is not just depression.

Mania, unfortunately, tends to mimic the same symptoms of stimulant narcotics that are especially attractive to young people. Cocaine, meth, and amphetamines all cause the person ingesting to babble, have delusions of grandeur, become outgoing/overconfident, need little sleep, and have endless amounts of energy.

There is no way to assess if the individual is genuinely suffering from Bipolar Disorder until they are separated from the narcotics and observed. Many patients find themselves misdiagnosed in their teens. Even adults regularly struggle to obtain a correct diagnosis.

Bipolar Disorder also has several symptoms in common with Borderline Personality Disorder and Schizophrenia/Schizoaffective Disorders. Symptoms of mania will often include hallucination and delusion.

We all exhibit the individual symptoms of mania from time to time. Phases of inspiration and motivation that just don't seem to last are typical. People consume caffeine and jabber—people who are nervous talk fast.

The biggest issue with early detection is just the nature of the beast. The first episode that usually presents in patients is a major depressive episode. This is why so many people with BP end up with a unipolar depression diagnosis.

There can be no diagnosis without some form of mania. Treatments for unipolar depression do not help those with Bipolar Disorder. So many sufferers end up in the office of a psychiatrist later in their life, confused with the way they have been behaving.

What is the point of early detection? Surprisingly, the answer is the number of years spent suffering from the illness. Sometimes, if Bipolar Disorder is caught and treated in time, the patient can actually delay the onset.

Psychologists are working with Interpersonal and Social Rhythm Therapy (or IPSRT), specifically for this reason. Their programs have been tailored toward young people to help slow the progression of the mental illness. Genetics and behavior are observed by the psychiatrists to determine if the child is a likely candidate for developing Bipolar; If yes, then the young adult is placed on a treatment plan.

Bipolar and Genetics

Throughout this book, we have learned that there is a genetic component to Bipolar Disorder. When psychologists attempt to diagnose patients with mental illness, they are screened with tests and questionnaires. The family's relationship to instability is also examined.

Doctors look for a connection to Bipolar on its own, as well as connections to other mental illness, or suicide. The risk of having BP increases ten times when a relative also suffers from a mental health disorder. Genetics are a factor in approximately sixty to eighty percent of Bipolar cases.

Bipolar Disorder already has a complicated relationship with genetics. Some psychologists believe that people are born with Bipolar. A significant event can act as a catalyst for the first episode, but the illness does not just appear out of nowhere.

Other doctors believe that Bipolar Disorder is more of a predisposition. Some people are born with a sensitivity to BP, and if their environmental factors align just right, then they develop the illness; in the same way, someone with heart disease is not born with the ailment but rather a predisposition toward it.

The doctors, as mentioned above, cite stress and loss as two of the most effective catalysts when it comes to setting off the Disorder. Bipolar can also occur as the result of a brain injury or because of basic brain structure. Substance abuse also has connections to the onset of Bipolar Disorder.

Age and Bipolar Disorder

Most of what we know about Bipolar Disorder comes from an adult perspective. We have learned that the first episode typically occurs before twenty, and rarely after thirty (with some exceptions). Some young adults go through their first episode right around the time they begin going through puberty.

Individuals that have their first episode right before or during puberty are usually also afflicted with an intense rapid-cycling version. We have also learned that it is challenging to diagnose young people, and if the Disorder is left alone, it will become more severe (too rapid cycling).

Symptoms of BP do not present the same in children and preteens as they do in adult counterparts. Younger individuals are way more likely to be diagnosed with ADHD or unipolar depression. In the future, doctors hope to be about to test the genetic material of the patient to find out if they have a mental illness.

As you already know, there are two different types of symptoms for this illness, depression, and mania. Children seem to run back and forth between these two categories much faster than adults.

Let's imagine that a child that has taken a sudden interest in drawing. He doodles all throughout his classes and then devotes his free time to filling sketchbooks. The child could be displaying early signs of BP, especially if this occurs more than once with multiple areas of interest.

Children also seem to exhibit euphoria by becoming goofy. The child may react to silly things that should not induce that sort of response. It can be easy to write kids off as just being happy, but this must be looked at in context with other clues.

Having a vivid imagination can also be a symptom of Bipolar Disorder. Children may play pretend for hours at a time or dream up stories and complex worlds. A child may become obsessed with their toys, developing personalities and backstories for all of their dolls or action figures.

Children also display a manic form of communication, babbling, and changing topics often. Pre-Bipolar kids may also lack the ability to sit through quiet activities like movies. Intense irritability can also be a sign that a child is on the path toward mental illness; they may throw fits and scream when they do not get their way.

Sleep is also an excellent indicator for children. A child who loathes taking naps and refuses to fall asleep during the night might be experiencing a rush of energy. Changes in the slumber can also serve as a warning sign that a new episode is starting.

Hypersexuality also grasps patients when they are relatively young. Children who include sexual themes when playing will dolls can be displaying early warning signs. Most adults would see this behavior as a troubling warning sign denoting abuse, so the behavior must be read in context to the rest of the child's actions.

Teenagers may also display a preoccupation with sexuality. Young adults may discuss topics that seem inappropriate in an obsessive way. Hormones drive teens toward being curious about sex, but pre-Bipolar individuals are much more intense with their interest.

On the major depressive side, a child might appear to often be sorrowful for no discernable reason. The same applies to teenagers. Instances that seem insignificant can trigger an enormous change in the affected individual's mood.

Depression can also cause changes in appetite, which could go in either direction. Some children/teens are more likely to eat their feelings for comfort, while others forget that they even need sustenance. A young adult's relationship with mealtime could be a clue to their future.

Excessive sleep can also be an indication that the child is on track to develop Bipolar Disorder. Teenagers notoriously sleep for a long time, but there is a point where the rest becomes excessive. If you are reading this book because you suspect that your child might be on the path to BP, buy a notebook, and begin to document the amount of sleep they achieve per night.

Sharing this information with a psychologist when the time comes can help to shed light on the situation.

Headaches, stomachaches, and other illnesses related to stress and depression can be a sign that a child or teen is ill. Young adults may also become very mopey, losing interest in all the subjects that they used to care about. Loss of passion is a sure-fire sign of depression.

Teenagers may often find themselves making suicidal comments. Phrases like "I wish I were dead" or "I want to kill myself" should be met with swift action. Therapy will not hurt, at the very least. Children and young adults don't always outwardly say how they feel, but with the correct lines of communication, their words could be heard before the situation becomes any more serious.

Gender and Bipolar

Bipolar Disorder is difficult, no matter the gender of the person with the diagnosis. There are also differences in every patient's experience with the illness. BP in children is different from the same condition in adults. The following sections will discuss if gender changes the experience. We will review the challenges for both men and women.

Women are more likely to have headaches, stomachaches, obesity, and thyroid disease related to Bipolar Disorder. Many ladies also complain of intense menstruation and possible PMDD. Period pain and intensity make sense with BP's connection to the internal clock.

There is a significant delay for both men and women, from the time they present Bipolar symptoms and the time they first receive treatment. Men wait approximately seven years before finding care. Women usually wait for eleven years before diagnosis and assistance.

Ladies are more likely to abuse alcohol while men typically turn to narcotics. Women also have a higher chance of displaying symptoms of anxiety and fear of social situations. Physical health issues are even more present in females.

Women are more likely to find themselves in the throes of a major depressive episode than men are, and for most ladies, this characterizes their first episode. Intense and early bouts of sadness could be why more females find themselves misdiagnosed by doctors as having unipolar depression.

Anti-depressants are prescribed by doctors to treat unipolar depression, but the medication is inappropriate for Bipolar patients; the drugs have the potential to trigger mood switching, and they often simply don't work.

Men face their own unique hurdles when it comes to Bipolar Disorder. Some of these discrepancies are accounted for by a difference in brain chemistry. Other trends paint are a result of the unfortunate way society portrays manhood.

As mentioned above, women are more likely to experience depressive episodes. Men tend toward having mania far more often than their counterparts. Guys are driven to aggression and agitation in these states, making their outbursts dangerous (in the legal sense).

Guys are not afflicted with as many symptoms of Bipolar as women, but their signs are much more intense. A stigma exists when it comes to men having mental health issues. Weird and unrealistic guidelines for masculinity often prevent men with Bipolar Disorder from reaching out and seeking the medical attention that they may desperately need.

Pregnancy

Bipolar Disorder is trying during the best of times. Many of the medications prescribed to stabilize patients are also harmful to pregnant women. Making the decision to have a child is a vast and life-changing moment for ladies with this illness.

For those who are making the decision to have children, research is the most effective way to prepare for the challenges that will present themselves.

The choice to rear children is ultimately up to the couple, but having a family can add so many complex layers to a Bipolar life. So many more opportunities for joy and contentment and a few new challenges will present themselves.

Pregnancy is famous for the hormonal havoc it wreaks on women. Moods change at lightning-fast speeds, and evidence shows that these emotions are even more potent for mothers with Bipolar Disorder. A thorough plan should be discussed with doctors before the gestation begins.

Some of the most commonly prescribed medications have the potential to damage the growing fetus. Lithium, the gold standard for BP medication, has been shown to cause heart defects in a small percentage of infants. Valproate carries the risk for brain defects.

Expecting mothers and their mental health professionals must have an honest conversation to examine the severity of the patient's symptoms. Stopping medication throughout the pregnancy is an option, but one that is not taken lightly. Halting drugs can mean that expecting women are left with only Therapy and self-care.

Another risk looms in the background, waiting for the big day. There rare is a condition called postpartum psychosis that mimics the more common postpartum depression. A couple of days following the delivery, the patient slips into either a manic episode or a depression.

One major difference makes postpartum psychosis more sinister than depression, and you have likely guessed it from the moniker. Hallucinations are extremely common for sufferers. The delusions cause an immediate danger to both mother and child, but emergency intervention can be used to protect both parties.

Breastfeeding can also be an issue for Bipolar mothers due to the medication that could potentially be passed through the milk. Infant formula is always an excellent option for those who are worried about passing on their drugs. Sharing the responsibility for feedings with a partner or loved one is ideal. People diagnosed with BP need their rest, and any change in the circadian rhythm can catalyze an episode.

The Twilight Years

Mental health professionals that work with elderly patients are already challenged. As the years have rolled on, the likelihood that the patient has accumulated more physical and mental ailments is strong. The interactions of medications are also something that doctors in charge of treatment must consider.

So many of the medications that patients are prescribed for BP have harsh interactions with other drugs. There is extraordinarily little research done on geriatric patients. The data that doctors use has mostly been taken from the observation of younger individuals.

Elderly people are much more prone to suffering from the harmful side effects of their medications. There are so few drugs approved for the treatment of geriatric patients when it comes to Bipolar Disorder. It is almost as if the entire demographic has been forgotten. Overwhelming evidence has shown that regular anti-depressants don't work for depressive episodes of bipolar.

Doctors are more than aware of this fact, but with no other medication on-hand to treat their patients, many of them have been forced to give out the anti-depressants. Many recommend starting low and slow and doing individual trials with the medicine in hopes that something might actually assist the elderly patient. Mania is much easier to treat throughout all age groups.

There is no research or verifiable data for maintaining a stable condition in elderly patients. Doctors are forced to improvise based on what works for younger clients. Science and medicine are currently failing the elderly in the area of mental health.

Lithium is still the most effective treatment for the elderly; it is also the most studied for the age group. Interactions are always an issue and must be carefully watched. There is also preliminary research that suggests the medication might help stave off dementia.

Hypersexuality

During manic phases, the individual with BP may have an intensely high libido. The word sex addiction has often been associated with hypersexuality. This is a unique aspect of Bipolar Disorder that presents very early in life.

Bipolar mania feels like pure energy. Not only *can* the afflicted person do everything, but they also *must*. The euphoric high makes people over-confident, social, loud, creative, and uninhibited.

Sexual desire, in a manic phase, has been described as an itch that can never be scratched. No matter how much intimacy or sex occurs, the need never dissipates. During the hypersexual manic episode, partners cheat and engage in risky behavior to try and satiate their hunger. Self-indulgence takes the top place on their list of priorities.

The Bipolar person will still feel guilty when they betray a loved one or become involved in something they perceive as undignified. Mania is not one giant party; it can ruin the mentally ill individual's life. Relief from the indulgences is only temporary, and the consequences of affairs and broken trust can last for an eternity.

Mania is such a force of nature that it can change the perception of the individual beneath its spell. A Bipolar person suffering from mania might see their actions as being justified in the moment.

Excessive masturbation can also be a sign that a bipolar person is becoming manic. When pleasing one's self takes priority over work or sleep, it has become an issue. Often, they become lost in a sexual fantasy world of their own creation, and they forsake interacting in reality; this can cause them to miss other obligations.

By recognizing when the mania is coming on, it can be treated by a medical professional. Sleep patterns, speech, and general energy levels can be an excellent indication. Hypersexuality can cause issues for Bipolar individuals, especially those in relationships.

Bipolar Love

The search for a dependable partner is high up on the list of most people's priorities. Humans are social creatures, built to crave intimacy and affection. Dating with a mental illness offers a unique set of challenges for all parties involved.

Depending on where the Bipolar person finds their potential partners, they are likely to run into ignorance.

Making the decision to reveal a diagnosis to a potential partner is both tempting and terrifying. There is no need to disclose private personal information on the first date. Getting to know the individual before divulging is smart. Right before defining the relationship is the best time to clear the air, prior to any commitment being made.

Commitment is a scary word for people who have been dealing with Bipolar Disorder for a while. Their relationships have a tendency to fail, and it has probably even been their fault, from time to time. Manic episodes are notorious for sparking affairs, cheating, and other risky sexual behavior, which can also frighten the non-Bipolar partner.

To maintain a successful relationship, the Bipolar person needs to be in an honest place with themselves. Ongoing treatment can help to assure that manic episodes and hypersexuality do not pose a risk to the new romance. Newly diagnosed individuals are a more daring choice because they have not yet had the time to learn to reel in more harmful behavior.

Partners with Bipolar do not want to hurt their significant other, and they aren't evil. Mental illness can convince people to do really out-of-character things, to satisfy their self-indulgence. BP individuals are usually sensitive, intelligent, and worthy, but they are occasionally compelled to act impulsively.

Bipolar significant others who have been in treatment for a while, and can control their mania, are lovely in relationships. Therapy teaches people to communicate all of their feelings effectively. Long-time sufferers are self-aware, passionate, creative, open, and efficient with communication. Meaningful partnerships are possible with those who suffer from mental illnesses, as long as both parties are careful and protective of one another.

Bipolar people are some of the most intelligent and creative individuals; they have gifted us some of the most impressive artwork mankind has ever known. BP is a mental illness that ramps up one of the most beautiful aspects of human nature, our emotions, until they work against the host, like a poison.

One day the stigma will completely vanish. One day there will be no more stereotyping. Bipolar people are capable of living long and fruitful lives, and they are worthy of love and compassion. Understanding is healing.

Conclusion

Congratulations! You have made it to the end of *Bipolar Disorder*. I hope that this book has offered you insight into Bipolar Disorder (or BP) and those who suffer from mental illness. History as not always been kind to those who are different. Even now, there is a stigma associated with being disabled. The more information that is consumed about the subject, the more the stereotypes die away.

Bipolar Disorder can be severe and complicated, changing the lives of the afflicted. Half of the adults with the illness are unable to work. Seventy percent have a relationship with substance abuse. Suicide is a considerable risk for BP sufferers. The severity of the condition makes education imperative, and we still have a long way to go.

Throughout this book, you have learned about all the resources for patients diagnosed with Bipolar Disorder. Cutting edge treatments with promising results cast a positive light on the future. Vocation Rehabilitation seeks to find jobs for those with BP, as well as helping those who need training for their career path.

The purpose of this book was to help those with Bipolar Disorder and to educate those who do not. I hope that you have found perspective, through this title, that you might not otherwise have come across. Finally, remember to not self-diagnose. If after reading this book you believe that you may be suffering from Bipolar Disorder, I encourage you to seek the assistance of a mental health professional to make an accurate diagnosis.

www.ingramcontent.com/pod-product-compliance
Lightning Source LLC
LaVergne TN
LVHW011738060526
838200LV00051B/3220